3/21

Goliath Frogs

by Grace Hansen

Abdo Kids Jumbo is an Imprint of Abdo Kids
abdopublishing.com

abdopublishing.com

Published by Abdo Kids, a division of ABDO, P.O. Box 398166, Minneapolis, Minnesota 55439.
Copyright © 2019 by Abdo Consulting Group, Inc. International copyrights reserved in all countries.
No part of this book may be reproduced in any form without written permission from the publisher.
Abdo Kids Jumbo™ is a trademark and logo of Abdo Kids.

052018

092018

 THIS BOOK CONTAINS
RECYCLED MATERIALS

Photo Credits: Alamy, Getty Images, iStock, Minden Pictures, Science Source, ©NHPA p.5,19/Photoshot

Production Contributors: Teddy Borth, Jennie Forsberg, Grace Hansen

Design Contributors: Dorothy Toth, Laura Mitchell

Library of Congress Control Number: 2017960565

Publisher's Cataloging-in-Publication Data

Names: Hansen, Grace, author.

Title: Goliath frogs / by Grace Hansen.

Description: Minneapolis, Minnesota : Abdo Kids, 2019. | Series: Super species |
    Includes glossary, index and online resources (page 24).

Identifiers: ISBN 9781532108235 (lib.bdg.) | ISBN 9781532109218 (ebook) |
    ISBN 9781532109706 (Read-to-me ebook)

Subjects: LCSH: Frogs--Juvenile literature. | Body size--Juvenile literature. |
    Animals--Size--Juvenile literature. | Animal behavior--Juvenile literature.

Classification: DDC 597.89--dc23

Table of Contents

Goliath Means Giant!

Goliath frogs are the largest frogs in the world! They are only found in the **rain forest** in western Africa.

4

5

Goliath frogs can grow to be more than 12 inches (30.5 cm) long.

7

If it stretches its legs out,

it can be more than 3 feet

(91.4 cm) long!

They can weigh more than

7 pounds (3.2 kg). That's as

heavy as some house cats!

Goliath frogs have big eyes!

Their eyes can be nearly

1 inch (2.5 cm) in **diameter**.

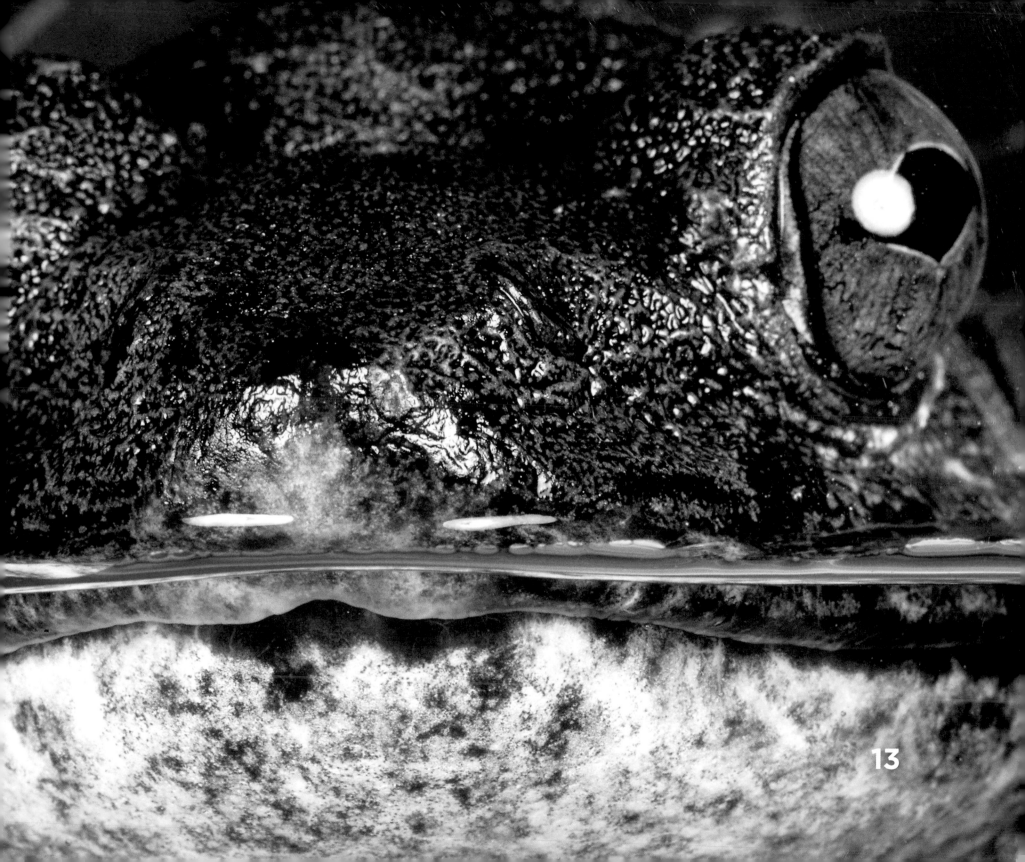

13

Goliath frogs have strong legs. They can jump more than 10 feet (3.0 m)!

15

Food

Goliath frogs sleep during the day. They come out at night to search for food.

Goliath frogs like to eat fish and other frogs. They even eat small **mammals**, like bats and mice!

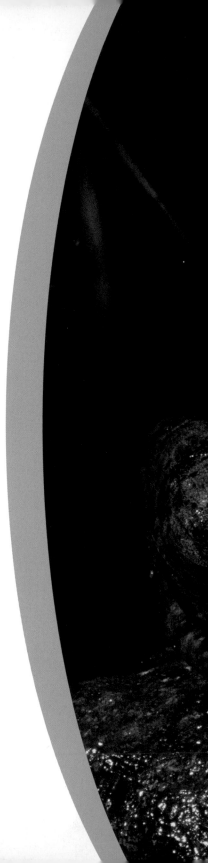

Baby Goliaths

Goliath frog **tadpoles** are the same size as other frog tadpoles. But they will grow to be huge! They can live for more than 15 years.

21

More Facts

- Male goliath frogs are larger than females.

- Goliath frogs do not make any noise. If they did, they would probably have a big croak!

- Goliath frogs have been around for a long time. They were alive when there were dinosaurs!

Glossary

diameter – the width of a circle, sphere, or cylinder.

mammal – a warm-blooded animal with fur or hair on its skin and a skeleton inside its body.

rain forest – a tropical forest with high annual rainfall and lots of plants.

tadpole – a young frog.

Index

Abdo Kids ONLINE

FREE! ONLINE MULTIMEDIA RESOURCES

Visit **abdokids.com** and use this code to access crafts, games, videos, and more!

Abdo Kids Code:
SGK8235

24